Science Builders

Learning about Rocks

by Mari Schuh

Consulting Editor: Gail Saunders-Smith, PhD

Consultant: Joanne K. Olson, PhD
Associate Professor, Science Education
Center for Excellence in Science & Mathematics Education
Iowa State University, Ames

CAPSTONE PRESS
a capstone imprint

T0050988

Pebble Plus is published by Capstone Press,
1710 Roe Crest Drive, North Mankato, Minnesota 56003.
www.capstonepub.com

Copyright © 2012 by Capstone Press, a Capstone imprint. All rights reserved.
No part of this publication may be reproduced in whole or in part, or stored in a retrieval system, or transmitted in any form or by any means, electronic, mechanical, photocopying, recording, or otherwise, without written permission of the publisher. For information regarding permission, write to Capstone Press,
1710 Roe Crest Drive, North Mankato, Minnesota 56003.

Library of Congress Cataloging-in-Publication Data
Schuh, Mari C., 1975–
Learning about rocks / by Mari Schuh.
p. cm.—(Pebble Plus. Science builders)
Includes bibliographical references and index.
Summary: "Simple text and full-color photographs provides a brief introduction to rocks and how they form"—Provided by publisher.
ISBN 978-1-4296-6072-3 (library binding)
ISBN 978-1-4296-7108-8 (paperback)
1. Mineralogy—Juvenile literature. 2. Rocks—Juvenile literature. 3. Minerals—Juvenile literature. I. Title. II. Series.
QE365.2.S38 2012
552—dc22 2010053933

Editorial Credits
Erika L. Shores, editor; Bobbie Nuytten, designer; Wanda Winch, media researcher; Laura Manthe, production specialist

Photo Credits
iStockphoto Inc.: dominiquelandau, 11 (top right), Nancy Nehring, 13 (left), Phil Augustavo, 13 (right), Stephen Morris, 15 (left); Photodisc, 9; Shutterstock: Anatoli Styf, cover, 1, Bork, 19, Cecilia Lim H M, 21, Douglas Adams, 7, Jan Kranendonk, 5, Michal Baranski, 11 (bottom), Ng Yin Chern, 17, Oksana Perkins, 15 (right), TTphoto, 22-23, 24, Tyler Boyes, 11 (top left)

Note to Parents and Teachers

The Science Builders series supports national science standards related to earth science. This book describes and illustrates rocks. The images support early readers in understanding the text. The repetition of words and phrases helps early readers learn new words. This book also introduces early readers to subject-specific vocabulary words, which are defined in the Glossary section. Early readers may need assistance to read some words and to use the Table of Contents, Glossary, Read More, Internet Sites, and Index sections of the book.

Printed in the United States 6024

Table of Contents

What Are Rocks? 4
Kinds of Rocks 10
Always Changing 20

Glossary 22
Read More 23
Internet Sites 23
Index 24

What Are Rocks?

Tiny rocks line beaches.

Tall mountains reach high in the sky.

Rocks are almost everywhere.

Where can you find rocks?

Rocks are solid minerals.

A mineral is something found in nature that isn't made by people, plants, or animals.

Earth is a rocky planet.
The crust is solid rock.
Below the crust is molten rock
called the mantle. Earth's core
is molten and solid.

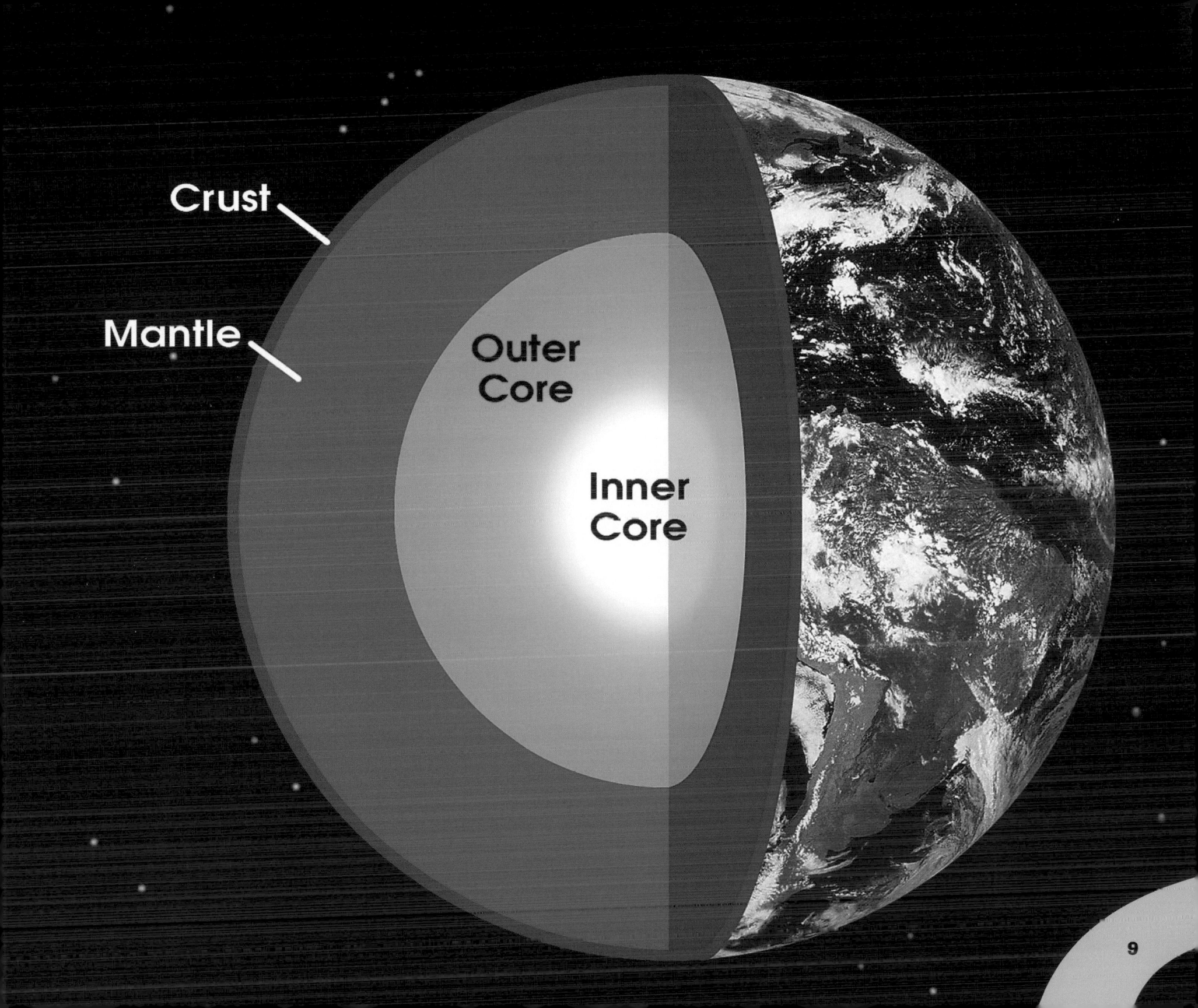
Crust
Mantle
Outer Core
Inner Core

Kinds of Rocks

Three main kinds of rocks
are found on Earth.
Igneous, sedimentary,
and metamorphic rocks form
in different ways.

igneous
sedimentary
metamorphic

Granite is a kind of igneous rock formed when magma cools underground. Obsidian is an igneous rock formed when magma cools above ground.

granite

obsidian

Layers of tiny rocks, sand, and mud build up over time. Pressure hardens this sediment into rock. Sedimentary rocks like shale and sandstone form.

shale

sandstone

Fossils are found in sedimentary rock.
Fossils are the remains of plants
and animals that were buried
in sediment.

MTCC

Metamorphic rocks are made from other rocks. Heat and pressure deep inside Earth can change rocks from one kind to another. Marble is a metamorphic rock.

marble

Always Changing

Wind, water, heat, and pressure slowly break down rocks. Rocks are always changing. In the future, the rocks around you could look different.

Glossary

crust—the outer layer of Earth

igneous rock—rock that forms when magma cools

magma—melted rock found under the earth's surface

mantle—the layer of molten rock below Earth's crust

metamorphic rock—rock that is changed by heat and pressure

mineral—a solid substance found in nature that is not made by people, animals, or plants

molten—melted by heat

pressure—the force produced by pressing on something

sediment—bits of rocks, sand, and mud that are carried to a place by water or wind

sedimentary rock—rock formed by layers of rocks, sand, or mud that have been pressed together